1 Samuel

At His Feet Studies

By Hope A. Blanton and Christine B. Gordon

19Baskets

1 Samuel: At His Feet Studies
© 2017 by Hope A. Blanton and Christine B. Gordon
ISBN 978-1-946862-01-3

19Baskets, Inc.
PO Box 31291
Omaha, NE 68131
https://19baskets.com

First Edition

Cover design by Sophie Calhoun

Photography by Rebecca Tredway

Contents

Study 1

Hannah's Desperation and Hope

Introduction to 1 Samuel

The book of 1 Samuel is an ancient book, with people we'll never meet in places we've never been. So why study it? First, some history.

Originally, 1 and 2 Samuel were one book, which was written and edited in several stages, the last of which was probably during the late tenth century BC. Though the Jews traditionally assumed that Samuel was the author of at least the first half of the combined book, there are many different opinions about who wrote this compilation, termed by Greek translators "The History" or "Book of Kingdoms."

Yes, it is an ancient book about ancient people, but these are not just any people. In 1 Samuel, the scope of history is narrowed down to focus on some very specific people within the nation of Israel. The Israelites were God's people, chosen by him for many reasons, including to bless all nations and eventually to provide the ultimate king, a savior not just for their nation but for all peoples. In our present day, the church is, in many ways, the equivalent or the continuation of Israel, the true Israel, God's people. In the most important sense, this is our history as the church, and these are our people. Hannah may have lived three thousand years ago, but she served the same God to whom we sing and pray and cry out. Samuel may have worshipped at the tabernacle instead of the local church, but he longed for redemption and the coming of Messiah, just as we do. This is part of the history of God with his people, which we continue in today. The geography, the year, and the culture have changed, but our God who sovereignly governs all creatures, nations, places, and events has not. And so as we read of his intervention, his answers to prayers, his usage of the day-to-day life of ordinary people to build his kingdom, we learn of him. We learn of his character, his lovingkindness, his provision, his discipline, and his protection of his people, which never fail. Our study of these foreign, faraway people and places is a study of our God, of his care for us, of his never-changing character.

What is happening in the life of God's people, the Israelites, as we begin 1 Samuel? In terms of redemptive history, the Israelites have taken parts of the Promised Land but have failed to obey God's commands completely. They have been led by Moses out of the wilderness and have been given God's law. They have conquered parts of the Promised Land under Joshua's brave leadership. They've been given judges to lead them in civil and military life. And yet their hearts tend more and more toward apostasy. Their desire and their need for a king has become clear. God used Samuel as a sort of transitional leader, the last of the judges but the first of the prophets. Samuel takes Israel from a republic of God to a monarchy (*Expositor's Bible Commentary*, 1 Sam. 1:1-18). He becomes the prophet who anoints the king and "holds the nation to the covenant" (ibid., 1 Sam. 1). Finally, Israel has a king. But for a king to be acceptable to God, he must be obedient to the word of God. And as we will see, even the best king, victorious in battle, leader of his people, chosen by God, is only a shadow, a broken but forward-looking picture of the true king who is coming.

Read 1 Samuel 1

Observation Questions

1. Who is introduced to us in this first chapter of 1 Samuel?

2. What is the tension between the two wives of Elkanah?

3. What is Hannah's conversation with the Lord in the temple? What is her conversation with Eli?

4. What results from her prayers?

Verses 1–10. As if being a barren woman in the ancient Near East were not hard enough, Hannah is doubly burdened by her mean sister-wife, Peninnah. Yes, she has a financially secure husband who clearly loves her. But the pain of Peninnah's words over the years and her own ache for a child reach a climax at this particular festival, which is probably the family's yearly trip to celebrate the Feast of Unleavened Bread, the Passover. Hannah knows from past years and from being a part of the small group of faithful people who actually still follow God's law that this is the place to speak to God. Shiloh is the place of the tabernacle, where the ark of the covenant rests, where God dwells and listens. Unlike the uninformed, distant, half-hearted piety we often assume of Old Testament saints, Hannah speaks to the Lord personally. Tears covering her face, she silently but fervently asks what she must have asked hundreds of times before: Please, Lord. Please give me a child. Hannah joins others who have desperately prayed these words in redemptive history: Sarah, Rebekah, Rachel, Elizabeth, and others. And though it is not always his choice to do so in the same manner, infertility is one of the places that the Lord often shows himself. As the commentator Dale Ralph Davis writes, "God's tendency is to make our total inability his starting point" (16). From Sarah comes Isaac; from Rachel, some of the twelve tribes; and from Elizabeth, John the Baptist. God answered these women not only with children but with children who played large roles in redemptive history. Their lives started as answers to the prayers of grieving, sometimes hopeless women.

Verses 11–28. Hannah acknowledges what would be true of the child she hopes for—he would belong to God. This is true for all of our children, but Hannah promises God that she would physically give the child back to him and that he would be a Nazarite. This vow included three things: refraining from intoxicating drinks, letting the hair grow, and avoiding all ceremonial defilement by corpses even of the nearest kin (Ellicott, 1 Sam. 1:11). Consider Eli's initial response to Hannah, and what this reflects about the general spiritual state of Israel. It's the Passover, the biggest yearly celebration of God's rescue of his people. In the most holy place where a woman could get the closest to God in her day, Eli's experience with God's people tells him that when he sees the state Hannah is in that she's most likely drunk. But Hannah humbly corrects the priest, asking for his blessing. The Lord remembers her, allowing her to conceive. And Hannah remembers her vow, promising to take Samuel back to the temple when he is weaned. Israelites tended to breastfeed about three years, at which time Samuel may have been initially been taken care of by one of the women who worshipped near the tabernacle (Keil and Delitztch, 1 Sam. 1:21). Among the ancients, women were generally employed in the office of porters or doorkeepers (Clarke, Ex. 38:8), so there were probably women already in service of the tent of meeting who could have helped raise Samuel. Hannah hands back to God the answer to her prayer, the son whose name means "heard of God."

Reflection Questions

5. When you read Hannah's story, what are some thoughts or feelings that come to mind for you personally?

6. What is beautiful about Hannah's pursuit of God with this desire for a child through prayer? What is scary about it?

Vulnerability, desperation, Surrender

7. Is this how we see our God, as one who loves to listen to hurting women?

8. Davis writes, "God's tendency is to make our total inability his starting point." This was true of Hannah's story; where has this been true of your story?

Many places —

9. What is your takeaway from watching Hannah give back Samuel, this child she longed and prayed for? What does it speak to your heart about?

Trustworthiness —

Reflections, curiosities, frustrations:

Study 2

The Lord Brings Low and He Exalts

Read 1 Samuel 2–3

Observation Questions

1. What are some descriptions of God's behavior that Hannah gives in her prayer?

2. What does Hannah take to Samuel each year when she and her husband go to offer their yearly sacrifice?

3. Describe the behavior of Eli's two sons. What are they doing that is displeasing to God?

4. What does the man of God in chapter 2, verse 27 say to Eli about Eli and his household?

5. What are some descriptions given of Samuel? How does God call him?

Chapter 2

Verses 1–10. Hannah worships at the temple, and as some translations read, her "horn" exalts in the Lord. The Hebrews were a shepherd people, and Hannah would have associated a horn, a favorite Hebrew symbol, with oxen and other animals whose strength lies in their horns (Ellicott, 1 Sam. 2:2). Hannah is not rejoicing in her own strength but in the Lord's, and specifically in the Lord using his strength on her behalf. Her entire prayer is a general warning to all self-sufficient boasters. Hannah shows us in this prayer that helping the weak, resourceless, end-of-her-rope, hopeless woman is simply the tendency of the Lord's ways (Davis, 22–23). She moves from her own life experience in verses 1–3 to God's general way of dealing with his people in verses 4–8 to his ultimate rule, which we will all see clearly. These smaller places in our lives, these little micro-salvations are foretastes, illustrations, scale models of his macro-salvation, which will eventually be on display and celebrated by all of his daughters. On the flip side, our places of self-sufficiency and pride are an offense to God, and they will be destroyed.

Verses 11–17. God had made provision in the law for his priests; they were to receive the breast and the right leg after the fat portion had been burned on the altar as a sacrifice made by the people. But the two sons of Eli are named appropriately here "worthless men." Instead of obeying the clear instructions given by God for every type of sacrifice, they mess with the sacrificial system and use their place of authority for their own appetites. We read later about more abuses of power, including having sex with the doorkeepers of the temple. They not only disregard the law; they steal from God by disrupting others' worship and taking whatever portions they want. These are two unbelievers left dangerously in a position of leadership among God's people.

Verses 18–21. Here we see God remembering Hannah over and over, but also remembering his people. Note the quiet words about Samuel in these verses that echo verse 11 and later verse 26. While Eli's sons seem to dominate the story, God is slowly growing his next leader. There is always reason to hope that God has something up his sleeve, some next step that we could not anticipate.

Verses 22–36. Davis makes two important observations from this section. First, a person can remain so firm in his rebellion that "God will confirm him in it" (Davis, 34). Eli's sons are unbelieving men whose father has failed to practice church discipline and remove them from the office of the priesthood. God has determined to destroy them and has told Eli such. Rather than trying to calculate the steps of the process and the timing of the hardening of a person's heart, we should tremble at the fact that our God has such power and that we are weak and fragile people. Second, "God will rule his people, if not through particular leaders then apart from them and in spite of them" (Davis, 37). It is a privilege, not a right, to be involved in and a part of the growth of God's kingdom. He chooses to use ordinary humans as the means through whom he encourages, speaks, teaches, and leads people to himself. But he does not need us as such and will do as he wills with or without us. His work does not depend on any particular person in history, save one.

Chapter 3

Verses 1–3. Samuel probably did minor jobs under the direction of Eli, like opening doors and so on. Notice that this is termed "ministry"—even small jobs at a young age. Though Eli is still at his post as priest in the tabernacle, there is no public or accredited prophet, no one person whom Israel can count on to speak God's word or determine his will (Clarke, 1 Sam. 3:1). This is probably a result of God's judgment for the corrupt leadership mentioned in the previous chapter (Davis, 42). God's word is a gift to us. The lack of his word, either because he withholds it as he does here or because people do not have ears to hear it, is the worst kind of famine.

Verses 4–10. Eli probably would have slept in a room built just off the tabernacle, and Samuel would have had a small room just next to his. Though he had spent the last nine years living in such a holy place and serving the Lord (Josephus tells us Samuel was twelve when God called him [Ellicott, 1 Sam. 3:1]), he had not yet known the Lord personally nor heard his voice. He was used to being called by Eli, his teacher. It takes Eli three times to figure out that the Lord himself is speaking to Samuel, probably from the most holy place, which would have been just beyond their rooms. Notice the Lord's patience with Samuel. His people are in a shambles, his priests having sex with all kinds of women and stealing big chunks of the sacrifice. He puts a plan into action beginning with a barren woman begging for a child. When the child is finally the right age, after years of serving under Eli, the Lord calls his name, and the child doesn't recognize his voice. But does the Lord chide him, get frustrated, sigh with exasperation? No. He waits for Samuel to figure out what's happening. He has time for Samuel to catch on (Davis, 45).

Verses 11–21. Imagine yourself as twelve-year-old Samuel, having grown up with Eli as your example, your father figure, your model. Your first direct word from God comes, and it is the judgment of this man, your teacher and human authority. While Samuel knows he will have to speak the truth to Eli, his compassion keeps him silent until Eli commands him to speak. This is always the tension for a prophet (or present-day preacher)—having to speak the truth about sin, generally or specifically, while also wanting to encourage and comfort. A true prophet will find himself or herself doing both. This is where Eli had failed. Though he confronted his sons, he failed to remove them from leadership. Because of their sin and his failure, judgment was coming. Everything Samuel predicted came true, proving his place as God's prophet. God had brought the famine of his words to an end; he was again speaking to his people through his own servant.

Reflection Questions

6. What phrase or part of Hannah's prayer sticks out to you or made an impression on your heart?

7. How is it possible for the two sons who were priests to be serving in the temple and yet not know God? Have you ever had this experience in the church?

8. Eli's reaction to the news that he and his household would not be atoned for because of his choices was, "It is the Lord. Let him do what seems good to him." What do you think your heart's response would be? Why?

9. Think about the story of how Samuel came to know God. Prayers of a barren mother, mentored by an ineffective priest, not knowing God for years while serving and living in his temple. How does this affect the way you view your own story of how God called you? How he might call your children or family or friends?

10. What was God's role in this part of Israel's story? What parallels are you able to draw with how he is currently working out his story in your life?

Reflections, curiosities, frustrations:

Study 3

God's Glory Departs

Read 1 Samuel 4–5

Observation Questions

1. What happens in the battle between the Israelites and the Philistines?

2. How does Eli die? What reaction does his pregnant daughter-in-law have to all this news?

3. What happens when the Philistines place the ark in the house of Dagon?

4. What places does the ark get moved to? What happens each time?

Chapter 4

Verses 1–4. It seems like the Israelites are always fighting the Philistines in some capacity. Have you ever wondered who they were? This people group, which appears in the books of Judges and Samuel, migrated across the Aegean and lived on the coastal plains of southern Palestine around 1200 BC (*ESV Study Bible*, 497). They are clearly organized and mighty in battle, killing four thousand of God's people in order to expand their territory. At this, the elders of Israel are confused. These elders are the supposedly wise, experienced group of tribal leaders entrusted with important decisions for Israel. And though they connect their defeat with a lack of God's presence, their correct interpretation of their circumstances stops there. Instead of repenting or asking why God has allowed their defeat, they immediately seek to use their magic charm of the ark to get what they want—victory. One commentator explains, "They vainly supposed that the ark could save them, when the God of it had departed from them because of their wickedness" (Clarke, 1 Sam. 4:3). It was the custom of all nations at the time to take their gods and sacred things with them to war. But Israel was not supposed to be like all nations. Israel was supposed to seek Yahweh, ask for his presence, follow his laws. At this point, God's people exhibit not faith but superstition. As Davis writes, "When we, whether Israelites or Christians, operate this way, our concern is not to seek God but to control him, not to submit to God but to use him . . . we are interested in success, not repentance" (54). Israel had become like the nations around them, parading the symbol of their God before them like a magic rabbit's foot. Is this the pattern of our prayers—asking God to sprinkle his magic pixie dust on what we've already determined to do? Or are we seeking God himself, asking him to give us ears to hear?

Verses 5-18. Thirty thousand men die, the army disbands, the ark is captured, and Eli's two sons die. Imagine yourself as the wife of one of these fallen men. Your husband and many of his friends are dead. The symbol of God's presence, the one tangible and continuous picture you have known to prove that the Lord was still among you and your people, has been taken into the camp of another tribe. The priest who has been presiding in the temple since you were born has just died. All reminders and assurances of your God's protection and provision have been taken away in the space of a day. The people of Israel must have thought it was over, that God had left for good. And yet this is the severe mercy of God. Severe in that many lives were lost, the honor of his name was lost among a pagan group of people, and Israel lived for a while in what must have been confusion and despondency. But even so, it was merciful in that Yahweh would "suffer shame rather than allow [them] to carry on a false relationship with him; and Yahweh will allow you to be disappointed with him if it will awaken you to the sort of God he really is" (Davis, 55).

Verses 19-22. Eli's daughter-in-law probably went into shock when all of the losses reached her ears. She "bowed," or literally "crouched," and gave birth, probably pre-term labor brought on by her shock. Notice that she, like Eli, is most concerned with the loss of the ark, naming her child Ichabod, which means "no glory" or "Where is the glory?" But, as H. L. Ellison asserts, she had it wrong: "The glory of God had indeed departed, but not because the ark of God had been captured; the ark had been captured because the glory had already departed" (51). God cannot be mocked.

Sometimes if his people are worshipping a caricature of him rather than the true God, he will remove himself so that we might seek him for who he truly is.

Chapter 5

Verses 1–5. In the Near East at the time, it was common practice to capture the enemy's god, proof that a people had been completely conquered. The Philistines would have understood that Yahweh had been overthrown along with his people and was now helpless. They place the ark next to Dagon partly as a way to prove their victory and Yahweh's defeat but also as vengeance. It was the temple of Dagon that had been destroyed by Samson when he asked God to strengthen him one more time so that he could move the two pillars supporting the whole building (Judg. 16:29). In pushing down the main supports of the building, Samson killed about three thousand people. The Philistines have not forgotten this act by a Hebrew. This is their chance to gloat, to be avenged.

Dagon was the main god of the Philistines and personified the prolific and bountiful principle of nature. He had the body of a fish (Dag, meaning "fish") and the hands and head of a human. They understood that all life came from this god. Therefore, they could not have anticipated what happened during the night, that their god would literally fall before the ark. The second time this happened, the Hebrew could be translated, "only the little fish was left to him," the least noble part of the image (Ellicott, 1 Sam. 5:4). What was left of this great god who had led them to victory against the mighty Israelites, who was supposedly gloating over the ark? Only the form of a fish, as its hands and feet worshipped the true God.

Verses 6–12. The Vulgate translates verse 6, "And he smote them in the more secret parts of their posteriors" (Clarke, 1 Sam. 5:6). Oh, dear. Because of the words chosen in other translations, we have reason to believe this was much worse than tumors. Most commentators suspect the people of Ashdod experienced bleeding hemorrhoids and severe dysentery. This would have been deadly in this time period, as there were no IV fluids or quick ways to hydrate the sick and dying. The Philistines finally make the right conclusion—they have not defeated the God of the Hebrews. The God of the Hebrews is actually presently defeating them. They consult their leaders, the lords of the five ruling Philistine cities, who tell them to send the ark to Gath, a city about twelve miles east of Ashdod. Same deal—more bleeding hemorrhoids. Next the ark travels to Ekron, where the people immediately beg that the leaders let it return to its own place. The Philistines have learned what the Israelites had not: the God of the ark cannot be manipulated or conquered.

Reflection Questions

5. The ark became a good luck charm or rabbit's foot to the Israelites. Have you ever done this in certain areas of your life with God? If so, how?

do the right thing = you'll be safe

6. Eli's daughter-in-law was grieved over the loss of the ark, God's presence. What specific things would be altered in your life if God's presence were removed?

7. What do you think God was communicating to the people by what he did to Dagon? Have you ever experienced such an extreme reaction in your own life as he deals with your false gods?

8. What is your reaction or thoughts about the tumors?

9. Neither the Israelites nor the Philistines clearly saw God as all-knowing, all-powerful, and the only wise God. How are you like them?

Reflections, curiosities, frustrations:

Verses 10-12. These are cows that normally had calves with them, who would never have been anywhere near Beth-shemesh. Untrained milk cows would not have been inclined to work together to pull a cart, and if they went anywhere on their own, it would have been to where their calves were (*ESV Study Bible*, 501). And yet they go straight down the road toward the Israelite city, even lowing (calling for their calves) as they go. The God of the ark, the sovereign and powerful Yahweh, reveals himself in this small way through the movement of a common milk cow. He both brings the ark back to his people and answers the Philistines in one bovine trip down the highway.

Verses 13-18. Beth-shemesh was one of the cities listed in Joshua 21 that was given to the Levites. Clearly, there is some recognition and joy in seeing the ark and even seemingly appropriate burnt offerings and sacrifices.

Verses 19-21. Verse 19 seems to come out of nowhere. The ark is back with the people of God, sacrifices are being made, a memorial is set up in Joshua's field to commemorate the day. Suddenly, bam! Seventy men are struck dead. Just for looking at the ark? But this was no casual looking. The language here indicates staring or even gloating, or perhaps inspecting. Rabbis through the ages have explained that some of the Levites probably got a little bit tipsy during the feast that accompanied the celebration of the return of the ark and decided to get a little too up close and personal with it (Ellicott, 1 Sam. 6:19). But like the Philistines before them, when God strikes them in judgment for their casual dealings with the ark, they do not confess or repent of their attitude or failure to give God the glory (weighty recognition) he deserves. They just try to figure out how to get rid of the ark. In our politically correct day, where God is often thought to be a familiar "friend," it is our temptation as well to push away the acts of God we find distasteful or illogical. But our God is other, unlike us, different. And as we saw in earlier chapters, he will correct his children rather than allow them to continue their worship of a caricature of the true God.

Chapter 7

Verses 1–4. It may seem that the action picks up again in verse 3, but don't miss verse 2; in this little verse sits twenty years of waiting. We have every reason to believe that during these years Samuel had been traveling on his circuit, "judging" all of Israel, as we read in verses 15–17 of this chapter. This was not legal judging or handing out punishments but more the work of "reproof, instruction, and counsel for living under Yahweh's Lordship" (Davis, 80). It is probable that God used this work of Samuel, the regular reminder of God's word and God's way, along with the oppression of the Philistines, to move the hearts of Israel to begin to cry out to God again. And so we read that Israel "lamented after the Lord." They ask, cry, and complain to God about the fact that although they (Israel) are in possession of the ark, the Philistines are clearly still a military presence and a nuisance to them. So Samuel tells them to do publicly what he senses is happening in their hearts, to put actions on their words—to repent. But to turn away from what? The Baals and the Ashtaroth were the male and female divinities of fertility worship of the Phoenician and Canaanite nations, respectively (Clarke, Judg. 2:11). Much of their worship, which promised the growth of crops, included orgies and even commanded religious prostitution. This kind of worship was an extreme temptation to the Israelites and had obviously become a part of their regular practice.

Verses 5–11. The pouring out of water before the Lord coupled with fasting would have represented a "repentant humble sinner bowed down in grief before the one true God" (Ellicott, 1 Sam. 7:5). Israel confesses their sin, and Samuel surely encourages them and instructs them in his "judgment." The people of Israel, pushed on by the suffering caused by the Philistines and the faithful ministry of Samuel, come to a place of repentance. Though there is much military action in the rest of this chapter, we must see that this is the central victory for God and his people in this part of their history.

Remember that many years may be condensed into a single sentence in this narrative. So the "then" in verse 5 is probably months or years after verse 4. During this time, the Israelites probably did the physical work of putting away the Baals and the Ashtaroth. This would have included destroying certain temples, stopping the use of prostitution for worship among Israelites, and causing a multitude of monetary shifts in the culture. These, coupled with a sudden gathering at Mizpeh, which means "watchtower," would have been red flags to the Philistine leaders, leading them to go to war against Israel (Ellicott, 1 Sam. 7:7).

Verses 12–17. This is not Samuel's first rodeo. He has been with Israel long enough to know that although this victory is an emotional high and that the people are sincere in their repentance, they will forget their God again. And so he puts up what was probably a pillar, and names it Stone of Help to remind the Israelites that their God has heard them, has helped them, and is faithful. We, also, need these reminders, pictures, stories, and symbols to remind us of God's faithfulness. We humans are fickle, weak, and forgetful. We need multiple reminders every week, even every day to recall the true character and real acts of God.

Reflection Questions

5. What do you think was the motive for the Philistines' attempt to send the ark back the way they did?

6. Are you surprised that God could guide the two cows back this way? Do you expect God to work in these ways? Why or why not?

7. Does the part of God that would strike down the seventy men for being inappropriate with the ark feel foreign to you? Why or why not?

8. What did repentance look like for the Israelites? How would you define *repentance*? What have you been repenting of recently?

9. Ebenezers are physical representations to remind us of God's help to us. What are tangible times that you have received God's help that you would like to commemorate? How could you physically represent the time you received this help from God?

Reflections, curiosities, frustrations:

Study 5

Israel Begs for and Receives a King

Read 1 Samuel 8–9

Observation Questions

1. What do the elders of Israel ask Samuel for? What is God's response to their request?

2. What does Samuel specifically warn the people a king will do?

3. What are the descriptions given of Saul?

4. How does Saul end up meeting Samuel? What is Samuel's response to Saul?

Chapter 8

Verses 1–9. Fear, worry, and anxiety can cause us to do illogical, ridiculous things that seem perfectly sane at the time. The last we heard of the Israelites in chapter 7, they had watched God throw the Philistines into confusion and win the battle for them. They regained all of the cities that had been taken from them and listened as their spiritual leader reminded them once again that it was God who had helped them. But time has passed. Maybe even years have passed. And Samuel's sons are not the dependable, righteous prophets their father had been. You can almost see the faces of the elders as they watch Joel and Abijah superintend as judges in Beersheba day after day, watch them taking bribes to settle a dispute instead of asking the Lord what to do. You can hear them as they sit together by the city gates, discussing what they might do. Who will govern us? Who will be our seer? Who will speak to God for us? Who will lead our army? The anxiety has built and the worry has multiplied as more and more of them agree, yes, something must be done. And so finally they confront Samuel, asking for a king. God's law had given permission for a king in Deuteronomy (17:14–20), so it's not that what they are asking for is sinful in itself, nor unlawful; but their motives are wrong. As Davis tells us, "After chapter 7 with its proper focus on repentance and deliverance, where her only weapon is prayer, Israel turns around in chapter 8 and makes the same error as in chapter 4; that is, trusting in some mechanical provision for her security. There it appeared as superstition ('the ark over us'), manipulating God; here it is political ('a king over us'), substituting for God. But it is the same idolatry" (Davis, 86). Isn't this like us in much of our own asking of things from the Lord? Is this not the bend of our hearts? Instead of simply laying our situation and need before God, we try to dictate what his help should look like. Israel does not want to hear the Lord's voice; they want to help themselves. And so the Lord will give them what they ask for and let them live the consequences (Clarke, 1 Sam. 8:22).

Verses 10–22. Samuel warns the people about what life under a king will look like. The long and short of it is this: slavery. Never before has Israel been subject to a king, but they know the stories of slavery from their ancestors. Samuel paints a picture of subjugation, taxes, and ultimately, suffering. But even his strong warning cannot be heard in the ears of these people who have decided they know the right way to resolve their fears. Good information, good teaching, and even great wisdom have no power to change without teachable hearts. Even here there could have been repentance, humility, and some sort of redemption. But Israel chooses to reject their true king and look for help somewhere else.

Chapter 9

Verses 1–2. Ancient peoples would have paid great attention to personal appearance and therefore would have appreciated the fact that Saul was handsome and a head taller than anyone around him. In the verses that follow, we are given other little clues about Saul, that his father is wealthy and that Saul is tenderhearted, as he worries about his father worrying about him.

Verses 3–14. At first the details of this passage may seem mundane, even irrelevant in the present context of finding a king for Israel. But through a prophet/seer and a long search for lost donkeys (which were the equivalent of the pickup truck on the modern-day farm and therefore extremely valuable), God answers his people in their request for a king. Isn't this the way God still sometimes leads his people? We wander through our days, simply doing what must be done—cooking, cleaning, shopping, driving children places, sleeping, teaching—and suddenly we find ourselves in the middle of a situation clearly arranged by God. Proverbs attests to this phenomenon as it reads, "The heart of man plans his way, but the Lord establishes his steps" (16:9). Saul and his servant think they are just on an errand for the farm, when really they are being sent to Saul's first phase of coronation as king.

Verses 15-27. But why would God go to such trouble? Isn't he displeased with his people asking for a king? The short answer is yes; he knows they are actually rejecting him as their leader. But, "Israel's stupidity cannot wither Yahweh's compassion" (Davis, 96). The Philistines, though defeated at Mizpah, have again become a problem for Israel. And while God clearly sees their idolatry in asking for a king, he also sees their suffering, hears their cries, and has compassion on them (verse 16). He prepares Samuel by "uncovering his ear" (verse 15), painting for us a picture of God pushing aside Samuel's head-dress and whispering something into his ear (Ellicott, 1 Sam. 9:15). The Lord reveals his plan to Samuel, a plan that is already in motion and that includes a searching Saul and his servant. These youngish men find themselves sitting in the seats of honor at a banquet given by the foremost spiritual leader of the land in a room that would have been attached to the place of sacrifice. This is, indeed, a solemn and important sacrificial meal. We see here the ridiculous and undeserved dignity bestowed by a holy God on his people. While they deserve punishment, he executes an elaborate plan for rescue. While they are pushing him aside in a search for help, he is whispering plans for an anointed one into his servant's ear. This is the persistent and tenacious love of God. In his kingdom, it is not tit for tat, you do good to me and

I do good to you. Instead, it is the love of the only perfect king who pursues, who protects and listens, who disciplines and parents as only a holy God can.

Reflection Questions

5. What is your response to the elders of Israel asking for a king? How do you see yourself in them?

6. What were some implications of having a king that you had not thought about?

7. Saul's journey to look for the lost donkeys resulted in him becoming king. Has God ever surprised you in such a way, redirecting you out of nowhere? When?

8. God pursued and accomplished a plan despite his people's waywardness. What is a word that you would use to describe this action?

9. What requests have you made to God that, like the Israelites' request for a king, indicate a rejection of his agenda for you?

Reflections, curiosities, frustrations:

Study 6

The Reluctant King Saul

Read 1 Samuel 10–11

Observation Questions

1. What things does Samuel do to proclaim Saul king?

2. What happens to Saul's heart? What does he do as a result?

3. How does Saul handle the news of the Ammonites? What is his plan of action?

4. How do the people respond to the victory?

Chapter 10

Verses 1–16. This may seem a curious ceremony happening at the beginning of chapter 10. Why is Samuel kissing this young man whom he only met yesterday? Why is the anointing being done in private? If this guy is supposed to be king, shouldn't more people know about it? Here we get front row seats into the private drama that is playing out first between Saul and Samuel. Consider Saul's past few days: He's still not exactly sure what's going on. Two days ago, he and his servant were just wandering around looking for donkeys. There was a big fancy meal and some conversation on the roof last night, but now he is headed for home and farm life as he knows it. Samuel sends the servant on ahead and pulls Saul aside for a private anointing service. He kisses him, not out of familiarity or love, but as a sign of reverence, paying homage to the one the Lord has chosen as leader for the people of Israel. Samuel's words match his posture as he tells Saul plainly that he has been chosen to be prince (leader) of Israel. Saul was a farmer, living what would have been a normal life of agricultural work, though comfortable because of his father's wealth. Imagine how he must have pondered Samuel's words during his journey home, wondering how this had come to be and what it all meant.

To encourage him and show him that this was, in fact, the doing of the Lord, Saul is given signs that all come to pass. In particular, he joins up with a group of prophets and prophesies among them, which likely means they were singing and worshipping God. At this time in Israel, there were schools set up for young men who were trained in loving and living pure and noble lives, a sort of higher education akin to seminary. These were probably not prophets like Samuel, through whom and to whom God regularly spoke. However, they must have regularly sung hymns of faith and would have been known to be set apart in their daily lives for this work (Ellicott, 1 Sam. 10:10). God has called a simple farmer to be king. And so he equips this farmer by giving him a new heart and sending the Spirit to enable him.

Verses 17–27. Samuel kind of looks like a party pooper in this situation. It's the public revelation of Israel's first king. Shouldn't they be celebrating? Well, yes and no. God has given them a king, but they shouldn't have asked for one. And as Davis writes, "Israel's God may love us too much to be nice" (107). Rather than smoothing over old mistakes and politely going forward with a proper ceremony where no feathers are ruffled, Samuel speaks the truth and reminds Israel, "You have rejected your God." He goes on to watch God publicly affirm what he had already done privately with Saul—choose the king and declare how kingship was to work in Israel. God even has to tell the people where to physically find their king, hiding, reluctant to assume his public role. It's as if we are to see, from the beginning, how dependent even the king is on the Lord to do any of his work. From his first call to his public announcement to every battle after, the king of Israel is never the ultimate authority. Even he is first and foremost under the authority of the Lord.

Chapter 11

Verses 1–11. The men of Jabesh know they are in trouble when Nahash comes to them. Jabesh was probably one of the farthest cities from the center of all of the Israelites and closest to where the Ammonites lived. They immediately try to talk terms with Nahash to avoid war. But Nahash's terms would effectively render the men of

Jabesh slaves. In ancient war, men typically held their shield with their left hand, thus shielding their left eye as well, using their right eye to fight. Gouging out all right eyes would mean they could never fight and would therefore be powerless, the equivalent of slaves. Clearly, the people have no hope when they hear the report from the messengers. In fact, the historian Josephus tells us that Nahash did, indeed, have a tradition of taking out the right eye of every Israelite that had ever come into his possession. These people of Jabesh have reason to fear.

Though Saul is king at this point, he is still working as a farmer, bringing his oxen in from the field when he hears the news. The saving moment in this entire narrative comes not in the fact that it is king Saul who hears the news but that the Spirit of God rushes upon him in that moment and directs the farmer to act like a king. This, remember, is the man who was found hiding behind the baggage at his own coronation. But under the influence of the Holy Spirit, he cuts his oxen into bloody slices, hands them to the men around him, and directs them to run to all of the different tribes of Israel in order to muster them to fight a terrifying and usually victorious king. This is the difference the Holy Spirit makes (Davis, 119). Think of the Christ-denying, hot-headed, uneducated fisherman Peter in the gospels standing up in front of thousands at Pentecost and clearly preaching the gospel. Think of Stephen, a Greek-born Christian chosen to serve widows as a deacon, standing up and preaching the gospel to the high priest, then asking for God's mercy on the men who were stoning him to death. This is what the Israelites were to see and what we are to see: God is your savior. It's not the king or the pastor or the Christian leader or the parent or the preacher or the good husband or anyone else through whom God chooses to work who saves you. It is God who saves you. As Jesus says in John 15:5, "I am the vine; you are the branches. Whoever abides in me and I in him, he it is that bears much fruit, for apart from me you can do nothing."

Verses 12–15. Gilgal would have been a well-known sanctuary of the tribe of Benjamin. Saul had already been made king, privately anointed by Samuel then publicly chosen by God in front of all of the tribes. What we witness here is a "solemn national confirmation of the...election at Mizpeh" (Ellicott, 1 Sam. 11:14). No longer will Saul be allowed to live a private farming life. Samuel at this moment calls the people to "renew the kingdom." The people are to once again commit themselves to the king chosen by their God, but more than that, they are to commit themselves to their God once more. This renewal was the pattern of the people of God then as it is now. We are continually renewing our commitment to God's kingdom and to his choices over our own.

Reflection Questions

5. Saul hid at his own coronation. Have you ever had an experience where you wanted to shrink from something God was asking you to do? Why?

6. The Spirit had a large role in these scenes with God's people. What did you learn about the Holy Spirit from this?

7. What is your reaction to how Saul's heart change came about? What questions does this bring up for you about God's ability to control hearts?

8. Farmer to king, God taking what isn't that special and doing the extraordinary. Where have you seen this pattern in your life or in the life of someone you know?

Reflections, curiosities, frustrations:

Study 7

Samuel Says Goodbye

Read 1 Samuel 12–13

Observation Questions

1. What things does Samuel bring up in his farewell speech?

2. What is the people's reaction?

3. What action from Jonathan and Saul reignites the conflict with Israel and the Philistines?

4. What does Saul do that Samuel rebukes? What results?

Chapter 12

Verses 1–5. We must set the scene before we dive into this passage. Samuel, God's gift to Hannah and her gift back to him, is standing before all of Israel, having faithfully served God literally his entire life. He is old and gray and has witnessed multiple generations and their love for and also rejection of their God. He knows that his time as the official prophet and leader of Israel is nearing its end and that Saul (who is probably standing with Samuel before the people) must daily serve in his royal capacity. Remember that this is the ancient Near East, a place where bribery and favors were as much a part of the economy of the day as sheep and cows. From the language here in verse 2, we can assume that Samuel has removed his sons from their priestly duties and authority and that they are now simply private citizens (Clarke, 1 Sam. 12:3). But while his sons had taken bribes and distorted justice, Samuel openly asks all of Israel to indict him at any point of his ministry. None can accuse him.

Verses 6–15. Samuel does here what all good leaders of God's people do throughout history: he recounts God's faithfulness in spite of his people's faithlessness. This is the cycle of God's people at all times in all places. We fail to obey; he loves us anyway. We forget about him; he remembers us. We go after other gods; he comes after us. This was Israel's pattern, and they had cried out to him directly for help over and over, until this last time. When they face Nahash, instead of asking for help from God, they ask him for a king, which is a rejection of God's leadership. Even so, in his mercy God promises to bless the people and their king if they all obey him and follow him. But he is clear about the consequences of disobedience.

Verses 16-18. The wheat harvest in this region happens between the middle of May and the middle of June. This is the dry season during which it is extremely rare to see precipitation of any kind. A thunderstorm on the day Samuel was speaking would have been like a snowstorm in Miami in April—not entirely impossible, but definitely shocking (Davis, 126). Remember the scene we set earlier. All of Israel is standing together outside, with their leaders before them. They do not witness this amazing storm from the quiet, dry safety of their living rooms; they are standing out in it. In the middle of the dry season comes pelting rain, thunder, and lightning. This gets the people's attention and scares them, which is the intention: to remind them of what they have done and with whom they are dealing.

Verses 19-25. See here the kindness and the severity of God. Like a father who sternly spells out the danger of the street in which his child is playing, God gets his people's attention to warn them of the danger of rejecting him and of hoping that something or someone else will keep them safe and happy. But the moment the people realize their sin, name it, and turn from it, see how quickly Samuel reassures them of the faithfulness of God! The people have had multiple warnings and chances to obey, and they have failed over and over. We would expect this section to be a public shaming of Israel by Samuel, recounting their repeated rejections of their provider. But no! Instead we hear Samuel saying, "Don't be afraid even though, yes, you have done these terrible things. Keep following the Lord. Know, respect, and reverence him. Consider him your master, and you his servants. Don't look for empty things to save you. The Lord will not leave you. He stays not because of your obedience but simply because he has chosen to love you." Is this not the gospel?

Chapter 13

Verses 1–7. Since we know the Israelites had no proper weapons for battle, Jonathan must have led some men and taken this military post by surprise. This is the equivalent of starting a war between Israel and the Philistines (Clarke, 1 Sam. 13:3). Saul calls Israel out to fight and finish what his brave son started.

Verses 8–15. On first reading, this passage may seem horribly cruel and excessive. Why would one mistake like this lead to God taking away the kingship from Saul? He does, after all, offer a sacrifice. Isn't he just trying to do the right thing when Samuel is late? The Philistines are ready to fight. The people are scattering. Seven days is an eternity when a nation is on the verge of a battle they're fairly certain they're going to lose. But Saul's actions reveal so much about his heart, and about what and whom he is really trusting. Charles J. Ellicott explains, "Saul considered that the people over whom he had been called to rule could, if necessary, do without this supernatural assistance" (1 Sam. 13:9). That's the bottom line. Saul thinks he can do what he needs to do without God. Saul has no authority to offer the sacrifice. He is the king, not a priest, and he has been given specific orders by Samuel to wait. Soldiers are leaving him, yes. But Saul has summoned his army to Gilgal, an isolated place where actual attack from the Philistine army is unlikely (Davis, 135). Samuel finally does come, on the seventh day just as he had said he would, though probably later on the seventh day than Saul would have hoped. The way Saul addresses Samuel exposes Saul's heart even further. He says to Samuel, "When I saw that the people were scattering from me, and that you did not come within the days appointed . . . " The *you* here is emphatic in the Hebrew; Saul is blame shifting. It's as if he says to Samuel, "Well, yes, I would have liked for you to have done the sacrifice, but you didn't keep your end of the bargain, so I didn't keep mine. I *had* to do it; *you* made me." The tragedy here is not that some battle ritual has been maligned. The real loss is that of the word of God himself. The prophet of God was to give the word of God, the instructions or guidance for this war. Saul, when pressured, makes it clear that he thinks he as king can function without God's guidance. Because of this, the kingship is removed. This will not happen instantaneously. Samuel is saying that instead of a whole line of kings coming from Saul, kingship in Saul's family will begin and end with him. God will give the kingship to someone who will rely on his word and his guidance instead of anything else.

Verses 16-23. As if we hadn't seen the helplessness and neediness of Israel clearly enough already, here we see their physical state of weakness. These men don't even have proper weapons. Here is confirmation of the desperate state of Israel; their physical vulnerability matches their leader's spiritual failure.

Reflection Questions

5. What areas of your life have you stopped asking for God's help? Why?

6. God showed his power and authority through a storm that probably felt extremely scary. Have you ever experienced God's power in such an intense way? How was it helpful to your heart? What thoughts came to mind when you read God's response to Israel's repentance?

7. Saul chose to take matters into his own hands instead of waiting on the Lord. Why and when have you done this?

8. What does relying on God's word and guidance look like practically?

Reflections, curiosities, frustrations:

Study 8

Saul's Rashness and the Lord's Rejection

Read 1 Samuel 14–15

Observation Questions

1. What do Jonathan and his armor bearer do to the Philistines?

2. What is Saul's response to Jonathan eating honey? What does he keep from happening to Jonathan?

3. What part of Samuel and the Lord's directions does Saul not follow?

4. What results for Saul? For Agag? For Samuel?

Chapter 14

Verses 1–23. When we last checked in on the Israelites, things were not going so well. Devoid of any proper weapons, the army, or what was left of the army, was following a king who already knew the kingdom would not transfer to his son because of his own disobedience and impatience. Saul and his men were waiting around, without much hope. Now, though, suddenly movement seems possible because of a devoted young man named Jonathan. Somehow in the household of his floundering father, Saul, Jonathan has grown a remarkable respect for and faith in God, which he puts into action here. While the others dawdle, Jonathan uses the imagination of faith to step out in tremendous hope. Looking at the same cliffs behind which all of the others are hiding, roughly named "Slippery" and "Thorny" (Davis, 142), Jonathan suggests to his armor carrier that they climb through these and confront the Philistine outpost head on, just the two of them. What would possess someone to do such a risky, unprecedented thing? "It may be that the Lord will work for us, for nothing can hinder the Lord from saving by many or by few." This is what moves Jonathan—the imagination of faith. Instead of stalling, he acts, hoping that God will use his actions in these circumstances to help save Israel. He doesn't presume upon God; it seems that he isn't sure this is exactly what God is planning to use. But he is so sure of God's goodness and power that he puts himself into a situation that he cannot fix, handle, or win on his own and waits for God to show up and fight for his people. God's response is absolutely overwhelming: first, two guards are defeated at the edge of the garrison, then twenty more are killed, and as if that weren't enough, there is a great panic and an earthquake, and the Philistines flee.

Verses 24–35. Saul doesn't want to take any chances. If the people stop to eat and refresh themselves, the Philistines might get away. So the king makes a stupid, self-defeating vow that weakens his own army, causing them to be faint with hunger. Further, when they do finally defeat the Philistines, they sin by eating the spoil (sheep, oxen, and calves) "with the blood." Obeying the Levitical law by letting the blood drain out of livestock before cooking or eating it would take time, and famished soldiers who had fought hard all day would hardly want to wait any longer to fulfill a religious rite. Saul tries to correct this problem by having them bring the animals to a central location for slaughter, but clearly he has acted unwisely.

Verses 36–52. The battle for the day is over; Israel has won. Against unbelievable odds, the Philistines are running. The feast is over, and it is time to rest. But Saul is not yet satisfied. He doesn't just want the Philistines to run; he wants them dead. Already Israel has taken their goods, their animals, and probably their weapons. Now Saul wants to keep pursuing until they are all wiped out, though the Lord has not commanded anything of the sort. The fact that no answer is given about whether or not Saul should go after the Philistines has nothing to do with the fact that Jonathan hasn't kept his father's silly oath. As Adam Clarke writes, "But why did not God answer the priest that day? Because he did not think it proper to send the people by night in pursuit of the vanquished Philistines. Saul's motive was perfectly vindictive: Let us go down after the Philistines by night, and spoil them unto the morning light, and let us not leave a man of them; that is, Let us burn, waste, destroy, and slay all before us!" (1 Sam. 14:42). Saul is not fighting the Lord's battle at this point. He is fighting his own bloodthirsty, greedy, angry battle. The Lord would neither be a part of the battle nor answer him. And yet, in his mercy God would use Saul in future battles to deliver Israel. By the standards of history, Saul was a successful king, victorious in many battles, strong, tall, handsome. God used him for a time to serve and protect his people. He was successful in general. About his enemies it is written, "wherever he turned he routed them." But remember, God has already taken the kingship out of Saul's line and has planned to give it to someone who would obey, no matter what. The success of Saul and the valiant men who were attached to him were not ultimately what God needed. For, "Yahweh is not looking for winners but for disciples" (Davis, 149).

Chapter 15

Verses 1-9. The Amalekites attacked Israel on their way out of Egypt, victimizing the weak and tired at the back of the group. God promised to completely destroy the Amalekites and avenge his people (Ex. 7:14). Four hundred years later, he gives the command to Saul, his king, who fails to obey.

Verses 10-23. This passage may evoke a reaction from us of "That's not fair!" or "Why so harsh?" Saul basically does what God asks and doesn't mean any harm in his slight variation on obedience. In fact, he uses what he doesn't destroy to worship. Doesn't that count for something? This is where the problem lies. Have you ever told a child to do something, given a specific command, only to have the child instead choose something else to do for you, while disregarding your actual request? "I didn't clean my room, Mom, but I did organize all of the books on my bookshelf." While we may appreciate our child's work on some level, in actuality he has been disobedient. We asked him to do something, to obey, and he didn't. He chose his version, his will.

With much higher stakes and much more to lose, Saul disobeys God. In truth, "All the smoke and fat on Gilgal's altar would never replace the pleasure God would have had from the living sacrifice of Saul's will" (Davis, 159). God doesn't want our own version of obedience or a half-hearted bow to him. He doesn't seek after extra-religious ritual or hope that we finally get all our prayers and decisions right. He wants our will; he wants surrender. And so he regrets (or even in some translations, "repents of") making Saul king. The word translated "regret" here always has an emotional element to it. It's not that God changed his mind. He is not fickle, but grieved. He is not flustered, but sorrowful. Our God is not a cold, emotionless despot, but a father who is somehow actually affected by his creatures (Davis, 161).

Verses 24-35. Saul seems to be more concerned about his reputation, and about the people continuing to see him and Samuel working together, than he is about defying the authority of the God of the universe. And so, with the kingship, the word of God, through Samuel, is also taken away from Saul. God has by this time already chosen a new king who would put God's will above his own, who would treasure God's judgment above that of any other man. God has rejected Saul as king in order to replace him with one who would obey and tend his people as a faithful undershepherd.

Reflection Questions

5. Jonathan presumed on God's power and goodness when he went to fight the Philistines. Do you think this was right or wrong? Why?

6. How did Saul's vow hinder his own agenda? Have you ever gotten so tunnel focused on a goal that you sabotaged yourself? When?

7. God wanted Saul's will and submission. God wanted Saul to trust his plans over his own. Where are you choosing your will over God's?

8. What do you make of Samuel hacking Agag to pieces?

9. God grieved over Saul ever being king. What does this description of regret change in your impression of God?

Reflections, curiosities, frustrations:

Study 9

The Lord Looks on the Heart

Read 1 Samuel 16–17

Observation Questions

1. What does God tell Samuel to do since Saul is no longer God's king?

2. How does Samuel go about finding David once he finds Jesse? What happens after David is anointed?

3. What is Saul and David's relationship like?

4. What is David's attitude toward the situation with the Philistine no one will fight?

5. What does David use to fight Goliath, and what results from this?

Chapter 16

Verses 1–5. Something like a dream must have died with Saul's failure, and not only for Saul but for Samuel as well. Samuel had lived through the people's rejection of the Lord as they asked repeatedly for a king, and he had reluctantly but faithfully anointed Saul. But hope must have grown through the months as Saul won battle after battle. There was such promise in this strong king. Samuel must have wondered if the kingship, or even Israel itself, would fall apart after Saul's failure. God interrupts Samuel's sorrow and tells him to move on—he has found another to serve him as king. God's kingdom doesn't fail just because one of his servants does. If he can use evil leaders like Pharaoh and Herod to accomplish his will, he can raise up a leader for his people when another disobeys. An elder's corruption, a pastor's failure, a deacon's mishandling of money, a staff person's misuse of power, all of these are reasons to grieve, but none are reasons to give up hope.

Leaders, teachers, and servants of God may come and go, fall and be restored, but his kingdom remains strong because "the true King never loses control of his kingdom" (Davis, 169).

The elders would have been nervous about Samuel coming to their town, thinking he was coming to "denounce judgments against their city" (Clarke, 1 Sam. 16:4). But Samuel simply calls them to sacrifice, telling Jesse and his family, who were probably the principal family in the area, to prepare themselves and help him get ready. They would have changed their clothes, washed their bodies in pure water, and prepared their minds to worship. After the blood had been poured out and the fat burned, the flesh would have been cooked and eaten (Clarke, 1 Sam. 16:3-4).

Verses 6-13. How revealing these verses are about human nature and how easily impressed we are by outward appearances. Even the great Samuel, the lifelong spiritual leader of God's people, would have chosen the wrong man. But God chooses unlikely people to do his will. David isn't even considered worthy of being brought for the viewing. But God knew what others could not yet see: David would obey and submit, qualities that made him a man after God's heart. And so the Lord commands Samuel to anoint David. To those standing around them, and even to David, this might have seemed to be just part of the ceremony of sacrifice. That is, they would have thought that Samuel was choosing David to assist him in the current sacrifice. But Samuel knew otherwise. David is given the Holy Spirit as well. Having been called to the office of king, he is also being equipped for the job. It is probable that from this time on David would have joined Samuel and his school of prophets to be trained in poetry and music (Ellicott, 1 Sam. 16:13).

Verses 14-23. We are surely meant to see the terrible contrast between the Spirit being given to David, God's chosen king, and the Spirit being taken from Saul. Commentators differ on their interpretations of the spirit who then torments Saul. Some name mental illness, some a demon, some simply a spirit of calamity or distress. Whatever it is, Saul has only the therapy of music to calm it, not the Spirit of God. On the other hand, David's musical ability is recognized at this point to the level that when a musician is needed, his service is requested. It would have been custom for anyone entering a king's service to bring a gift to pay homage. Therefore, David is sent to Saul bearing gifts. Saul is comforted by David, who probably would have remained his servant and armor bearer for a time before returning to Samuel. The irony here is clear. David is the true king, though at this point even he doesn't know this. He has been anointed the first time but only to enter a period of testing, training, and humility. The chosen king is sent to serve the sinful, broken, rejected leader who has failed. He goes willingly, not yet being revealed in his full office, to serve the one who will later hunt him, stalk him, and even try to kill him. Even here in the very earliest stages of David's service in the kingdom, we see a type and a shadow of another king, who would be anointed and filled with the Holy Spirit, then immediately led into a season of testing by the Holy Spirit. This is often the pattern of the leaders of God's people; they are called, equipped, and tested, usually in painful and lonely ways in order to prepare them for the weighty call of caring for the bride of Christ.

Chapter 17

Verses 1-11. Fast forward about eight years from David's anointing. Gone is the earlier bravery and victory. Absent are any words about Israel consulting God about this battle. God's people are mocked every day by a bully, Goliath. Notice how his physical stature distracts both armies, just as that of Saul's and Eliab's distracted Samuel earlier. True, Goliath would have been quite overwhelming, probably standing at about nine feet nine inches, wearing armor weighing about 150 pounds. He had clearly battled personally to determine the fate of all of the Philistines before, and has obviously always won. Israel is scared and frozen.

Verses 12–40. Meanwhile in Bethlehem, life goes on mostly as usual for David, tending and protecting sheep, until his father sends him on one of his regular trips to check on his brothers in the battle. Imagine the contrast for David. One day he is leading sheep to drink and singing new songs to God, trying out a new melody as he walks along with the flock. We can picture him spending hours in the fields, meditating, praying, forming his prayers that would later become the Psalms as he leads and carries sheep. Then suddenly he is among the armies of Israel, listening to a Philistine mock his God. This is the important, repeated word in this chapter, more noticeable in the Hebrew: *mock*. We read it first in verse 10 from Goliath—"I defy"—then in 25, 26, 36, and 45. It is translated "reproach" and "defy" but could also be "mock" or "deride." The giant is not just jeering the army or playing the bully; he is ridiculing, taunting, provoking, and insulting the God of the army, David's God. This is what shocks David and motivates him to act. Notice who always gets the credit in David's speech for all of his talent and success. He basically gives Saul a record of God's faithfulness and explains that he believes God will continue to be faithful, helping him win this fight just like he has others. Notice also that everyone David confronts considers David too weak. His brother is annoyed by him, sneering. Saul tells him he is too young. Goliath tells him he is puny (Davis, 188). But David knows it is not his own strength or record he is relying on.

Verses 41–58. And so comes one of the most loved scenes of the Bible. The twenty-something kid (probably twenty-two or twenty-three) uses a two- or three-inch diameter stone (which, because he has had much practice killing lions and bears that were common in Palestine at the time, is nearly as fatal as a bow [Davis, 187]), swings it around and flings it (probably at a speed of 100 to 150 mph), killing the giant. But what we usually miss are the words around the action, which are just as important as the action. David is not the hero, and our job is not to "be a David" or to "beat our Goliath." Yahweh is the hero. David is a small, younger brother sheepherder who is probably four feet shorter than Goliath. Though he clearly has some slingshot skills, his confidence is in Yahweh's adequacy, not his own. The thrust of the story here is not Look, Israel found someone good enough! The crazy story here is that God uses an underdog, a youngest child, a questionable dreamer who is too green and untested to even wear the right protection to beat the opposing army's champion. The point is that Yahweh will not be mocked. He will win. And he will use the most unprecedented, weak, surprising person you could imagine to do it. Why? Because it gives him glory. Because it increases his reputation. Because when he uses the weak, there is no question about who actually has the power.

Reflection Questions

6. The Lord had to remind Samuel that "the Lord sees not as a man sees; man looks on the outward appearance, but the Lord looks on the heart." In what relationship in your life currently have you been looking on the exterior and why?

7. What is your reaction to David, the privately anointed king, having to serve Saul when the evil spirit from the Lord tormented him? In what ways could this be used to test and equip David?

8. The mocking jeers of the unbeatable giant were upsetting to David. When have you encountered God being mocked?

9. David had such confidence that God would deliver Goliath into his hand because David came in the "name of the Lord of hosts." Do you see this as being naive or having faith? Why?

10. God was glorified by his young sheepherder David killing Goliath with just a small river stone. What picture of God does this paint for you?

Reflections, curiosities, frustrations:

Study 10

Jonathan and David's Deep Soul Friendship

Read 1 Samuel 18–19

Observation Questions

1. Describe Jonathan and David's relationship.

2. What are all the things that make Saul jealous of David?

3. How does David end up marrying Michal?

4. What are the different ways that Saul tries to kill David? What are some things that prevent this from happening?

Chapter 18

Verses 1–5. Our picture of Jonathan is filled out a little more here and takes a turn we wouldn't expect. Remember that Jonathan was the one who in chapter 14, verse 6 took the initiative against the Philistines while the rest of Israel, including his father, Saul, were sitting around waiting for something to happen. Jonathan led his armor bearer through a treacherous valley in the hopes that God might work on Israel's behalf. This courageous man of faith was the prince of Israel, the soon to be king. Standard behavior for his day and age would have included trying to kill any competitors for his throne, as well as their offspring. But Jonathan sees in David something more valuable and exciting to him than a future of power; he sees a man who loves God, and a man through whom God acts. He sees courage and confidence in the Lord. And so Jonathan commits himself to David and generously gives him all of the emblems of his own power. Jonathan's chief desire is that God's will be done and that he be given glory. This affection for God's will and faith in who God is crowds out any selfish ambition or vain conceit and frees him to be generous with his own position, wealth, and future. Isn't this what can make us free as well? As S. G. DeGraaf writes, "This deed on his part was an act of faith. Only faith makes us willing to be the lesser. Faith causes us to surrender the rights we pretend to have over against the Christ, who is truly Israel's king" (qtd. in Davis, 194).

Verses 6-16. The contrast between Jonathan's freedom to serve and Saul's crippling jealousy is obvious here. Saul is met by a sort of victory parade as he returns from battle. At this time in Israel, it was principally the women's job to celebrate victories, sing at funerals, and in general commemorate important events. But in this instance the women's song does more than just memorialize a victory. It highlights a growing sentiment in Israel regarding who is favored; David is a bigger winner than Saul. This has to be Saul's biggest nightmare coming true. Years have passed since Samuel told him that the kingdom had been given to another. How many hours has Saul spent wondering who this new king might be? He must have looked for him, considering each warrior, each singer, each young man who showed any talent at all. As Ellicott writes about verse 10, "This dread expectation of ruin and dethronement had been a powerful factor in the causes which had led to the unhingement of Saul's mind. Was not this gifted shepherd boy—now the idol of the people—the future hope of Israel?" (1 Sam. 18:10). Saul rages and pouts in verse 8, "What more can he have but the kingdom?" Saul is still groping for power, trying to hold onto what God has taken from him.

Verses 17-30. Remember that Saul was supposed to have given his daughter to the man who beat Goliath a long time ago. Instead Saul uses his circumstances to try and have David killed. These are the murderous thoughts of a man who has become irrational and psychotic in his jealousy. The more he has attempted to sabotage the Lord's anointed, the stronger and more loved David has become.

Chapter 19

Verses 1-9. The time of secret plots and covert operations to have David killed are over. Saul is now openly instructing his son and his servants to destroy David. David's first deliverance comes by God using Jonathan to talk Saul out of his foolish plan. But Saul's jealousy has grown to the point of madness, and the next period of David's life will be a constant flight from Saul.

Verse 9 has proven to be tough for biblical scholars. Translators have used "evil," "harmful," "tormenting," and even "spirit of sadness" to convey the meaning of the spirit upon Saul. The first thing we must make clear is that this spirit, however we describe it, is from the Lord. Evil or good, all things must have not only the permission but also the government of the sovereign God to affect the world. Here, as in other places in scripture, God uses an evil spirit for his own purposes. Remember that before Job began his plunge into the depths of despair because of all of his losses, God presented Job as an example of faith to Satan, who then received God's permission to take away everything except Job's life. These are not rogue spirits who roam the earth outside of God's command. Even they are limited in their power by the true king. As Ellicott explains, "Why certain souls should have been exposed to this dread experience is, of course, beyond our ken. From the scanty information vouchsafed to us, it seems, however, that the power of the evil spirit was sometimes permitted to be exercised (a) as a trial of faith, as in the case of Job; or (b) as a punishment incurred by the soul's desertion of God, as in the case of Saul" (1 Sam. 19:9).

Verses 11-17. Here David is delivered a second time, again, ironically, by a family member of Saul. It is suggested by many commentators that this may have been the occasion for David's writing of Psalm 59. Notice that Michal, like many other Israelites, seems to consistently possess idols of some kind. These idols vary in size, from the small gods that Rachel concealed by hiding them in her camel seat and telling Laban that she was on her period and couldn't stand up to the one mentioned here, which was probably life-sized. These were probably seen as protective or guardianlike deities, kept in the house as bringers of good fortune to the family

(Ellicott, 1 Sam. 19:13). Here is the future king of the nation of Israel, sleeping with a wife who keeps idols around the house for extra help. This sort of idolatry is clear and easy to spot. Our idolatry, as citizens of the kingdom who live in the twenty-first century, is often much more subtle.

Verses 18–24. Again God delivers David from his enemy. But unlike what we would expect, God intervenes and personally prevents David from being destroyed. David has fled to Naioth to seek the company and protection of Samuel. But three times God prevents David's capture and death by overcoming the messengers and eventually Saul himself with his Spirit. Consider the diversity of God's deliverance and the protection of his anointed. God will use whatever means necessary to execute his plan. David was an exceptional man in exceptional circumstances, for sure. Though our role in redemption is much more modest, we worship the same steadfast, faithful God who will accomplish his will in our lives. This means that he will also use for us and for our sanctification any means necessary.

Reflection Questions

5. Have you ever experienced such an intense loyal friendship as that of David and Jonathan's? Describe it.

6. What is striking to you about the difference between the way Saul was described when he was first introduced in scripture in 1 Samuel 8–9 and now?

7. What are your thoughts or responses to the evil spirit from the Lord that tormented Saul?

8. Saul was haunted by his jealousy over David's success and fame. David was haunted by Saul's constant attempts to kill him. Where in your life have you been persistently haunted by something?

9. Deliverance for David came over and over in many forms, the last of which was God's Spirit. What is your reaction to this pattern in his life? How have you experienced a variety of forms of God's deliverance?

Reflections, curiosities, frustrations:

Study 11

The Protection of David

Read 1 Samuel 20–21

Observation Questions

1. What do David and Jonathan plan together to do in order to determine if Saul still wants to kill David?

2. What is Saul's response when David does not come to the table for the second day?

3. What are the things Ahimelech the priest gives to David?

4. What happens to David when he encounters Achish the king of Gath?

Chapter 20

Verses 1–11. It seems there were some of God's laws the Hebrews had actually kept. According to Numbers 28, they were to offer sacrifices and have a feast at the beginning of each month. These months would have been lunar months, counted from new moon to new moon. Though the Mosaic law specified the sacrifices were to be done at the tabernacle, the last tabernacle had been destroyed at Shiloh. Therefore, they were probably held at tribal centers, hosted by the primary family in the area (Ellicott, 1 Sam. 20:5). It sounds from the text like David is fairly sure Saul is planning to kill him at the feast. David plans to be absent as a way to test out his suspicion and prove to Jonathan what he knows to be true. Several things could make a person unclean according to the Mosaic law and could prevent him from attending a feast like this. But both David and Saul would have known that being unclean would only delay a person by one day. David deliberately stays away long enough to force Saul to inquire about his absence.

Verse 8 can easily be missed in the midst of all of the action and suspense of this story, but it is the key to the entire chapter. Remember that back in chapter 18, verse 3, Jonathan had made a covenant with David. The Hebrew language explains the making of a covenant in terms of cutting. This is the same language God used when he "cut" his covenant with Noah in Genesis 6:18 and also with Abraham in 15:18. Read Genesis 15. By causing a smoking fire pot to pass between the halves of dead animals, God basically said to Abraham, "May my body be broken like these animals if I fail to keep this promise to you." This is the weight of a covenant—death. It is a binding contract, a promise made with blood. Also important in this transaction of covenant is the word *hesed*, "lovingkindness," though that is a fairly wimpy translation. A better one is found in the *Jesus Storybook Bible*, where *hesed* is described as, "a Never Stopping, Never Giving Up, Unbreaking, Always and Forever Love." *Hesed* is, according to Davis, a corollary, or analogy, for *covenant* in the economy of God (206). David and Jonathan know this language of covenant and lovingkindness because it is the language that God uses when giving his promises to his people. This covenant is a promise and a place of safety, a refuge or sanctuary in the midst of danger or hopelessness. These two God-fearing, God-loving men would not have used this language flippantly but are making a contract with each other on which their very lives depend. When David asks Jonathan in verse 8 to "deal kindly" with him, he literally asks for *hesed* from Jonathan, based on their covenant.

Verses 12-23. Why does Jonathan suddenly ask for mercy from David in verses 14-15? It is clear to Jonathan that David will soon be king, and he fears for the lives of his own children. As Ellicott writes, Jonathan asks David to go against the custom of the day and "the fate which too probably awaited them, it having been in all ages a common custom in the East, when the dynasty was violently changed, to put to death the children and near relations of the former king" (1 Sam. 20:14). Jonathan knows very well what all the surrounding kings do when power shifts from one family to another. He is asking David, as the leader of God's people, to be different, to have mercy.

Verses 24-42. Two things become obvious in this text, as David begins the difficult season where he runs for his life from Saul. The first we learn from Jonathan. Living as a disciple of the kingdom is all about emulating the king. As Davis writes, "True life does not consist in securing 'you and your kingdom' but in reflecting Yahweh's faithfulness in covenant relationships" (212). Doesn't this just cut across the grain of what we hear from the world every day? Letting go of our "rights" is hard and feels like death. Jesus knew this when he said in John 12:24-25, "Truly, truly, I say to you, unless a grain of wheat falls into the earth and dies, it remains alone; but if it dies, it bears much fruit. Whoever loves his life loses it, and whoever hates his life in this world will keep it for eternal life." We live for someone else's kingdom, not our own.

The second thing that jumps out of this text is the word peace. It seems crazy that Jonathan could say to David in this situation, "Go in peace." But the peace that he offers is a peace that comes from the covenant between the two of them. Both are committed to God's kingdom and whatever it might bring. As Davis writes again, "The Christian then does not have peace because things are peaceful. He has peace because a greater one than Jonathan has pledged his friendship to him" (213).

Chapter 21

Verses 1-6. The first place David seeks safety is in the sanctuary, seeking the help of the high priest, Ahimelech. The priest is probably not being unfriendly but cautious, as it would not have been the norm to see David, the proven warrior and son-in-law of the king, traveling alone. David's speech to the priest may have been his attempt to protect Ahimelech from being implicated in aiding the enemy (Davis, 217). David is on the run and in need of food and weapons. The showbread was, by God's law, to be twelve loaves set out every day, one loaf for each of the twelve tribes of Israel, and was only for the priests to eat. But as Jesus alluded to in Mark 2:25, this was a place of necessity, therefore making the eating of the bread an act done without sin.

Verses 7-9. This is where David's plan for refuge in the sanctuary breaks down: Doeg is there. We are not sure why Doeg, the servant of Saul, was "detained" at the sanctuary. He could have been fulfilling a vow, staying for some sort of purification, or a number of other reasons. But once David realizes that he has been seen by this man, he knows that he is no longer safe at Nob.

Verses 10-15. It quickly becomes obvious in this passage that David doesn't understand the extent of his fame following the slaying of Goliath. Achish is Goliath's hometown, the very worst place David could have gone for sanctuary. Perhaps he thinks that the leader of these people will be impressed by the number 2 man of Israel coming to join forces with Saul's enemy. But the leaders of these Philistines have a very different reaction. David's reputation proceeds him in the songs of the women. By the time he realizes his mistake, it is too late. Verse 13 states that he was "in their hands" and probably means that he was "under arrest, confined, and taken into custody" (Davis, 219). Acting crazy is David's attempt to escape, and it works. The people in the ancient Near East often considered insane people in some way possessed, or at least under the protection of some sort of deity, and therefore undesirable.

From the headings in the Psalms, we understand Psalm 34 to have been written during this time that David was running for his life from Saul. Notice that it is not David's brilliance, planning, holiness, or courage that brings his deliverance. David is foolish, desperate, and confused (Davis, 219). The Lord, however, is not. As David wrote about this part of his life in Psalm 34:19, "Many are the afflictions of the righteous, but the LORD delivers him out of them all." And in verse 4, "I sought the LORD, and he answered me and delivered me from all my fears."

Reflection Questions

5. How would you explain the covenant that David and Jonathan formed in order to preserve both their lives?

6. Jonathan and David had such an intense bond that stemmed from Jonathan's selflessness and service. What effect do you think this had on David?

7. Who in your life has been a Jonathan to you? Describe how that friendship has changed you.

8. Read Mark 2:23-28. In the context of what Jesus said about this moment in David's life, what can we assume about the priest Ahimelech's heart?

9. Here is "king" David running scared and pretending to be mentally ill. Is this your definition of leadership? Why or why not?

Reflections, curiosities, frustrations:

Study 12

David Becomes a Fugitive

Read 1 Samuel 22–23

Observation Questions

1. What does David's family do when they hear of his troubles?

2. What happens to the priest that "helps" David?

3. When David is still on the run in chapter 23, what does the Lord ask him to do?

4. List some of the different places Saul pursues David to kill him. What happens at the end of chapter 23 that allows David to escape?

Chapter 22

Verses 1–5. And so begins David's life as a fugitive, living in a cave with his extended family, who are probably afraid of Saul's anger as well. Discontent is spreading throughout Israel as Saul's melancholy increases. The men who join David are dissatisfied for a variety of reasons but clearly have put their hope in David doing something about it. He does not turn them away but organizes them. Here we must not picture a band of fugitives cramped together in a dark, small cave. These were enormous caverns, sometimes adorned with arches and huge rooms. Imagine connected openings, each the size of a large hotel lobby. This would have been a dry, safe refuge for such a group of people. Some of these caves are still used by shepherds today for themselves and their animals.

David's parents would have been of great concern to him, as the life of an outlaw was dangerous and uncomfortable. Why would the king of Moab oblige him so readily? Though the text does not explain, Davis reminds us that David's great-grandmother was Ruth, the Moabitess. It is possible that God, in his *ḥesed* (lovingkindness), had arranged this very place of refuge for David's parents one hundred years before, when he chose Ruth to carry on the line of this earthly king. As Davis writes, "Yahweh plans his kindnesses long beforehand" (222). The prophet's advice to leave and go to Judah may also have been God's care for David.

Verses 6–10. Note the paranoia and insecurity that rule Saul's mind. Those he accuses are his closest advisors, his extended family, his friends. Saul trusts no one, thanks no one, aligns himself with no one. The sad king exposes his own tortured psyche by his words in verse 8, "None of you is sorry for me." He imagines himself totally alone and defenseless, even as his servants stand around him. This is the dismal consequence of months and years of nursed jealousy and bitterness, unchecked by repentance or contrition.

Verses 11–23. It would not have been unusual for Ahimelech to inquire of the Lord for David. And this action would have been perfectly appropriate, as David was the king's son-in-law. Saul, in an act of unchecked madness, orders the guard who stood around him to kill the priests. These guards were literally runners who ran by the royal chariot as an escort (Ellicott, 1 Sam. 21:17). While they were obviously loyal to Saul, they would not lift their hands against those who wore the linen ephod—those who had a right to administer sacred things. Doeg, the non-Israelite, has no such hesitation. He and Saul bear full responsibility for this slaughter. Notice, however, that they are fulfilling the clear prophetic words of the Lord in 1 Samuel 2:27-33. Read those verses. The Lord had warned Eli that the discipline for his sons' abuses would be severe. God is not asleep, unaware, or surprised by the slaughter of his priests. In fact, he uses Doeg and Saul to carry out his will. As Davis writes, "Even in opposing God's kingdom God's enemies only bring to pass God's word" (228).

Chapter 23

Verses 1–5. It was a common practice of many people in the ancient Near East to steal from the threshing floor, where the grain was separated from the inedible chaff, during the harvest. But David does something unexpected when he learns that the Philistines were robbing other Israelites. King Saul was clearly failing in his responsibility of protecting his people. David could have easily blown off the news about Keilah or even aligned himself with the Philistines to get back at Saul. But instead, in a moment of true leadership and self-forgetfulness, David employs his army and influence in the service of his brothers. This is the action of a true king, although he is not yet recognized as such.

Verses 6–14. Notice that David, through Abiathar, has access to God and his word, while all Saul has are his growing delusions. Saul is so deceived in his own thoughts that he thinks God is actually on his side and that David is the one that has been abandoned. His words in verse 7 could also be translated, "God has rejected him" (Ellicott, 1 Sam. 23:7). Access to God's guidance through the appointed priest was and is still the ultimate need and privilege. Though it is in a different context, this is same benefit that we, as believers, enjoy now (Davis, 238).

Verses 15–18. Jonathan shows up just at the right time. He doesn't bring another army, inside information, or military strategy. Jonathan brings the encouragement of God's word. He reminds David of what everyone somehow seems to know—that he will be king and that he is in God's hand.

Verses 19–29. God allows the hunt to get so, so very close. Saul and his men are literally on one side of the mountain, while David and his men are on the other. Saul is closing in, ready to pounce, thrilled at the prospect of finally destroying the object of his jealous obsession. David is running for his life. The king and all of his power are so close that one wrong turn, one slow pace would mean the end. Imagine the fear, the dread, the adrenaline of David and his men. But suddenly, what should God use for the salvation of David but the Philistine army! How often do we in our prayers prescribe for the Lord his method of help for us, when all along he has planned some incredible and surprising source of assistance that so much more gloriously displays his supremacy and control of any and all circumstances?

Reflection Questions

5. God knew that David would be concerned about his parents as he lived life as a fugitive. God used this Moabite connection of Ruth from decades before to provide the very protection needed in this moment for David and his family. Do you believe that God could have or would have prepared something so specific like that? Have you seen places in your life where you have walked into a kindness of God that was clearly prepared long beforehand for you?

6. Saul's years of nursed jealousy and bitterness ultimately left him broken down, feeling alone, deeply insecure. Where in your life have jealousy and bitterness left their fingerprints in negative ways?

7. There is real evil done when Saul kills the priest out of anger. However, God used this sinful action of a human to fulfill his promise. How can these both be true? Was only God really responsible? Or Saul? Or is it both?

8. Saul, the father, could not be more different than Jonathan, his son. What consistent patterns do you see in each of their individual lives that led them to such different ends?

9. At the end of chapter 23, God's provision for David's escape from Saul was, oddly, the Philistine army. Tell a story from your life when you have tried to control the Lord's method of help for you, not knowing he had something different planned to display his supremacy and control.

Reflections, curiosities, frustrations:

Study 13

David Shows Mercy

Read 1 Samuel 24–25

Observation Questions

1. What happens in the cave where David is hiding when Saul goes in to relieve himself?

2. What is the conversation between David and Saul about?

3. Describe Nabal. What does he do to David? What happens to him?

4. Describe Abigail. What does she do for David? What happens to her?

Chapter 24

Verses 1-7. Will David grab at what has been promised to him by the Lord, or will he wait until the Lord hands it to him in his own time? That is what is on display in chapters 24-26. David knows the kingdom will be his but that God has not yet given it to him. Saul is officially still the king and is again coming after him. David and his men have made their way to En-Gedi, a beautiful oasis in the desert where he and his men can escape the large army that Saul obviously has thought necessary for the final capture of David. The scene here seems confusing until we consider again the caves of the region. The "sheepfolds" described here were actually small semicircles built up around the mouths of very large caves. They were created with loose stones and thorns to protect the sheep from predators. During storms and at night, the shepherds would put their sheep into the large caves for further warmth and protection. Those inside the cave, once their eyes had adjusted, could easily see animals or people who came and went out of the entrance, where the sun was bright; but looking into the massive expanse of the cave, one only saw thick blackness (Ellicott, 1 Sam. 24:3). Saul is exhausted after his pursuit of David and walks a few paces into the cavern both to relieve himself and to lie down for a few hours. David's men, hidden in the recesses of the cave, consider this God's way of handing Saul into David's hands for destruction. And for a moment, it seems that even David is tempted with the opportunity to end the whole thing once and for all. He hears the voices of his men whispering into his ear, feels the adrenaline rushing through his body. All he has to do is pick up his sword and do the deed. But the evil of his intentions strikes his heart and he stops himself.

Saul, no matter what his terrible actions, is still the Lord's anointed, the one chosen for this specific time to be king. David knows that his time has not yet come. Taking the kingdom by force would be outright disobedience to the Lord. What an amazing moment of testing, which David thankfully recognizes. What looked like unqualified opportunity for revenge was actually temptation. These two things—opportunity and temptation—can often look strangely similar. Jesus was tempted in this way by Satan in the desert, declining the temptations to use his power to escape, hurry up, or slightly modify God's will. As his followers, this is the temptation we often face as well. As Davis writes, "It is the temptation of the short cut….We sometimes long to find a 'key' or a major 'breakthrough' or a decisive 'insight' that will place our Christian living on some kind of higher plane where we are almost always above hindrance, frustration, and despair….How we yearn for a short cut around the arduous, wearing, time-consuming labor of sanctification" (248).

Verses 8-22. Saul, not the most emotionally stable character in the book of 1 Samuel, relents in a moment of tenderness. But he has not forgotten the words of the prophet in chapter 15, verses 23-28. He knows that the kingdom will soon be taken from him. And so he asks David to spare his descendants the terrible death that was common for children of overthrown kings, just as Jonathan had requested earlier.

Chapter 25

Verses 1–8. An era has ended; Samuel is dead. The faithful man who served the Lord from the time he was a toddler probably into his nineties, anointed the first two kings of Israel, began the prophetic schools of the time, and kept himself completely from corruption (1 Sam. 12) is gone. But the Lord has not left Israel to fend for herself. He is testing and training her next leader, this time not through a king but through a fool. The name Nabal literally means "foolish" or "villainous." And *caleb* in Hebrew means "dog," so the description of Nabal as a Calebite also carries the implication of "doglike." This man is a brutish, unreasonable, ill-tempered ass. But he is rich and probably married to this wise, beautiful, perceptive woman only because of his wealth. It was and still is the norm for wandering groups of people in this region to steal provisions and animals from the flocks of shepherds (Clarke, 1 Sam. 25:7). In contrast to this, David, who still has a large band of men traveling and living with him, protects the sheep and the men from others who would exploit them. A request for a share of the provisions when it came time for the celebration that would have accompanied a sheep shearing of this size would have been a totally reasonable request from David and his men.

Verses 9–17. Nabal's response indicates that he is of the faction of Saul, and that he hates David (Ellicott, 1 Sam. 25:10). Not only is he stingy and cruel; he is a political adversary. For David, this means war. With four hundred men in tow, Nabal's house doesn't stand a chance. We get the feeling from the interaction of the servant with Abigail that this is not the first time they've had to navigate around Nabal's preposterous actions.

Verses 18–31. Though he has been wronged, David's reaction here is disproportionate and sinful. He saw clearly and stopped himself when he had the chance to take vengeance into his own hands with Saul. But here David is blind with anger, and he is about to do to the whole household of Nabal exactly what Saul had done to the city of Nob. Enter Abigail. This wise woman humbles herself and reminds David of what he already knows to be true—the Lord is on his side. Her boldness and quick actions are what the Lord uses to stop David. The phrase she uses in verse 29, "the life of my lord shall be bound in the bundle of the living in the care of the LORD your God," is one of the earliest references to the idea of eternal life. It comes from the idea of "packing up in a bundle articles of great value or of indispensable use, so that the owner may carry them about his person" (Ellicott, 1 Sam. 25:29). Abigail is telling David that his life will be carried around on the person of God himself.

Verses 32-44. Nabal is terrified when he realizes the danger he so narrowly missed. He probably refused to eat and died quickly. The doglike, stupid, extremely rich man is dead, just like that. David admits his hot-tempered decision and his need of Abigail's discretion. Notice that David gives the credit to the Lord in verse 32. Left to his own devices, the future king would have acted exactly as the rejected king, but the Lord interrupts his shortsighted plans. Instead of destroying Nabal and his servants, he stands by while the Lord kills Nabal. Then David marries Nabal's beautiful wife and therefore, according to the laws of the day, ends up owning everything that had been Nabal's. God prevents David from carrying out his own plans and rescues him in the process. Isn't this often the way that the Lord protects us? Perhaps sometimes when we feel frustrated that our carefully laid plans fail, we should consider that the Lord may be delivering us from unknown pain.

Reflection Questions

5. What David did to Saul displayed such deep humility. What was your reaction to him choosing submission over vengeance?

6. Davis writes, "It is the temptation of the short cut....We sometimes long to find a 'key' or a major 'breakthrough' or a decisive 'insight' that will place our Christian living on some kind of higher plane where we are almost always above hindrance, frustration, and despair....How we yearn for a short cut around the arduous, wearing, time-consuming labor of sanctification." Where has this quote been true in your life?

7. Abigail showed kindness and wisdom in the face of her husband's foolish and unreasonable behavior. How would you characterize her as a wife?

8. David had been so astoundingly gracious to Saul but then turned around and was rash with Nabal. Recount a time when you were kind to someone who greatly wronged you, only to quickly snap at someone who hadn't.

9. These two chapters display so many types of human behavior. The repentant king, the gracious and hotheaded future king, the foolish, harsh husband, and the wise, responsive wife. What do these things tell us about human behavior in complicated life situations?

Reflections, curiosities, frustrations:

Study 14

Mercy Gives Way to Brutality

Read 1 Samuel 26–27 and 1 Samuel 28:1–2

Observation Questions

1. What does David do to Saul when he finds Saul encamped in the wilderness? How does Saul respond?

2. What things does David say to Saul about the Lord in chapter 26, verses 23–24?

3. Why does David take his family and soldiers to live in Gath with Prince Achish?

4. What does David spend his time doing while living there?

Chapter 26

Verses 1–12. Once again the rejected king is hunting the future king, this time with five times the number of men David probably has with him. It was common at the time for the person of rank to lie at the center of the troops while all of the wagons or carriages were circled around him for protection. This is how David sees Saul—surrounded and sleeping. Abishai whispers the same temptation that David's men had suggested in chapter 24, "Let me kill him! The kingdom can be yours now! Don't you see that God has given him into your hands, that this is your opportunity? Let me strike him once. I won't need to do it again." But David is not the same man who cut Saul's robe while in the cave. Nor is he the same man who went after Nabal in a plan to destroy him and all of his relatives. Instead of walking into the temptation to grab at the kingship, David this time exhibits, as Davis writes, a "deeper patience, a more informed restraint," and he is learning that the Lord can be trusted to "handle both fools and oppressors when such matters are left in his hands" (270). As we see in verse 10, David has moved his imagination from the crafting of a story where he forces his own ascension to the throne to a story where the Lord himself takes care of the obstacle of Saul. He reasons that either 1) the Lord will just kill him, 2) he will die of old age, or 3) he will die in battle. David is content to leave the choice in the hands of God. In the meantime, he and his man take from Saul's head the spear, the emblem of power and kingship (Clarke, 1 Sam. 26:12).

Verses 13–25. The fact that David is able to creep so close to the king is a failure of Abner and his men, but it is also an encouragement for David. It is the Lord who put the men surrounding Saul into a deep sleep. What must it have done to David's heart to hold the sword of Saul and to sneak out of the camp so easily? Samuel had anointed David, but years have passed since that scene. He has been chased, hidden, and hungry; he has acted as a madman, been betrayed by the Ziphites, and been pushed out of his own country. In verse 19, David voices some of his sadness at his current circumstances. Though he clearly understands that he can talk to Yahweh at any location, he cannot visit the tabernacle or worship with the people of God while on the run in various caves and hillsides. He tells Saul that it is as if he has been told, "Go, serve other gods." David, the musician, the one who loved to sing songs long before he was ever in the service of the king, must have longed to be among God's people in worship. And the Lord knew the heart of his servant. He knew that he needed encouragement, and so he offers it in the form of the king's sword in his own hand. As Davis writes, "Yahweh tends to be that kind of God, one who reaches out to his tired and wearied servants and in the midst of their discouragement grants them some plain token, some small evidence that he has not forgotten his word and promises to them" (273).

Chapter 27

Verses 1–7. The first verse of this chapter may strike us as a sudden shift, a change in David's thinking. How does David come to this conclusion? God has intervened time after time: he kept him from acting foolishly with Nabal, encouraged him through Jonathan, and even gave him Saul's spear as a reminder of the kingship that had been promised to him. But in verse 1 we read David's state of mind: he is convinced Saul will eventually kill him, so he decides to seek refuge with former enemies, the Philistines. Isn't this the same despair we sometimes feel? We may feel confused by David's despondency after seeing God's saving hand in the pages of scripture, and it may be disappointing to see David's failure after chapters of such restraint and trust in God. But David was human, just like us. He constantly feared a violent death. He was tired, tested, and homesick. It seems that the men of his army had wives and families with them, depending on him, looking to him for safety and decisions. And so David, in a period of discouragement, fools Achish. While this king sees David as an ally in his war against Saul and his territory, David takes the opportunity to fight the nomadic enemies of Israel in the southern region of Judah, lying the entire time to Achish.

Verses 8-12. There is more reason to be disappointed in Israel's future king. While living in the city of Ziklag and lying to the king of the Philistines, David's raids take on an extremely brutal character. Any survivors of his invasions could easily tell their stories to others living in the area, and word would eventually get back to Achish, thus blowing David's cover. And so David kills, and kills and kills. Children are killed. Old men and women are slaughtered. We and the Israelites following him may have begun to be tempted to trust in this powerful, courageous, anointed king for ultimate redemption, but as David's sin and brokenness is more and more clearly revealed, we are reminded again of the true king of whom David only serves as a type. There is only one king who never fails, never lets discouragement change his path of obedience, never forgets who orders his steps. We only see glimpses of this glorious king in the life of David.

Chapter 28

Verses 1-2. Achish has every reason to believe that David has broken all ties with Saul and has been his ally for the past several months. Therefore, when the time comes for the real offensive to start against the armies of Israel, Achish has no problem assuming that David and his men will go into battle with him.

Reflection Questions

5. Because God put Saul and his army into a deep sleep, David was able to steal Saul's spear. Again, without the Lord's help David's plans would have failed. What things can you actively do in your life to draw your attention to all the hidden ways the Lord helps you daily?

6. In chapter 26, verses 18–20, we read that one of the implications of Saul's constant pursuit of David is that David has not been able to worship with God's people. What effect would not being allowed to weekly attend church and worship with God's people have on you?

7. David seemed to have every right to kill Saul and two opportunities to do so, and yet he didn't. It says a lot about his humility before the Lord. Define humility. In what areas of your life do you long for more of it?

8. David seemed to have a deep trust in God at times, but at other times, he resorted to forming his own plans for protection. In what situations recently have you vacillated between these two tendencies?

9. Chapter 27 tells of a deep, destructive season in David's life. This is the man who wrote the words to so many of our treasured Psalms. What does this tell us about God's ability to use these weak, dark seasons in our lives?

Reflections, curiosities, frustrations:

Study 15

Saul's Desperation Grows

Read 1 Samuel 28–29

Observation Questions

1. Saul removes mediums from Israel. Why does he go and seek one?

2. Who appears when the medium calls on a spirit? What does he say to Saul?

3. When David and his men show up for battle what is the Philistines' reaction?

4. What does King Achish say to David when he sends him away?

Chapter 28

Verses 3–9. We already know from the beginning of chapter 25 that Samuel has died. The author here is not giving us new information but setting the spiritual leadership context for what is about to happen. There is no proven, trusted prophet in the land. The man to whom Saul had gone multiple times for guidance is gone. Although his spiritual advisor is absent, his responsibility is not. Saul is seeking God in all of the ways he knows how. He asks God to speak to him through dreams, but no dreams come. He inquires through the high priest and the Urim, a tool used to ask for guidance. None comes. He consults the prophets, probably from the school of prophets Samuel had established. None can give him a word from the Lord. Responsibility for the lives of many people and their well-being while an army is mounting a significant offensive is one level of stress, but responsibility like that with no answer or guidance from the Lord is terrifying. This desperation is what pushes Saul to the frenzied place of asking for a medium, which he had previously outlawed in accordance with God's law. What makes the situation doubly sad is that guidance about what to do is not Saul's biggest need. Saul needs communion with the Lord, restoration, reconciliation. Once again he is chasing something good from the Lord instead of the Lord himself.

Verses 10–19. This woman lived in a time when people in her line of work were routinely found out and killed through a network of informers. Her fear is merited, as any customer could have betrayed her. It's interesting that Saul reassures her, swearing by the name of the Lord, whom he is betraying, that he will not betray her. Saul reasons that if the Lord won't talk directly to him, he will find someone who will, even if that person is dead. Apparently mediums at this time used something called a "familiar," some sort of spirit who would aid them in bringing up a departed soul. It is clear from the surprise of the woman that her regular "familiar" does not appear. Instead, she is shocked at what she sees. This is not her regular practice nor her regular informant. It seems that instead of the woman bringing up Samuel, Samuel surprises her and apparently identifies Saul. Samuel's words give no more hope than any of Saul's other attempts to ask for guidance. It may seem confusing that Saul actually succeeds in speaking to Samuel, who tells him the truth. Does this connection condone the use of mediums? It doesn't. We have to remember that scripture condemns the use of mediums not because they don't work but because they are wicked.

Verses 20-25. Literally, Saul falls the entire length of his body. The woman, who probably removed herself from the immediate scene during her first shock, returns when she sees the once dignified king in such a pitiful state. She attends him, killing the fattened calf, preparing a meal for Saul truly fit for royalty.

Chapter 29

Verses 1-5. The Philistines have not forgotten about David and how he defeated Goliath so many years before. They know whom he had been fighting for and therefore how odd it is that he is marching with them into battle against his former allies. Notice that in this chapter it is mostly Achish's words that fill the space. He vehemently defends David, recalling his loyalty since defecting from Saul. Achish trusts David and believes his stories of Judaic victory for the months prior, but the folksongs sung by Israelite women about David that originally angered Saul are still making their way through the Philistine camps. These men are approaching one of the biggest battles in Israel-Philistine war history, and they are not ready to trust a man who could easily turn in the midst of combat and give his old king, Saul, the best prize of all.

Verses 6-11. It seems that Achish almost feels guilty telling David that he can not fight for him. David, of course, has to act the part and pretend he is incensed by Achish's declaration. At Achish's insistence because of the other Philistine leaders, David relents and leaves with his men. End of story. That would be the way an outsider would have told the tale, as that is how all events appeared to Achish and his men. But we know more; we know the one who is writing history. As Proverbs 21:1 reads, "The king's heart is a stream of water in the hand of the LORD; he turns it wherever he will." David has worked himself right into a corner. He will have to betray either Israel or Achish. And yet at just the right time, in a way that allows David to keep his honor and his life, God intervenes. Again. As before, God uses the Philistines as the way of salvation for his own future king, leading him right up to the edge of sure disgrace and then rescuing him. Only God could do such a thing. Only he could orchestrate such a situation. Who knows what David's prayers must have been like leading up to the day of the battle, how desperate they must have been, how confused. Even he could not have anticipated such a delivery. God not only provides deliverance from situations of injustice and evil consequences of the sins of others; unbelievably, God sometimes provides deliverance from the evil consequences of our own sin and bad choices. David walked right into the fallout of his own decisions. God would have been completely just if he had let him live through the disgrace he deserved. But God is, by nature, a rescuer, a promise keeper, a deliverer. He salvages lives and plans and kings right at the places where it is most clear that redemption could come from no one else.

Reflection Questions

5. Saul was desperate to get guidance form the Lord, but every avenue was silent. Have you ever experienced this? What did it drive you to do?

6. In a bizarre scene, we see Saul using a medium to bring Samuel back from the dead to speak to him. What are your reactions to this moment?

7. Saul seems to consistently be missing the heart of God. Why do you think that is?

8. How do you reconcile David creating a false identity to Achish and never coming clean about it? If David went to your church, would you be friends with him?

9. God not only provides deliverance from situations of injustice and evil consequences of the sins of others; unbelievably, God sometimes provides deliverance from the evil consequences of our own sin and bad choices. When has God graciously protected you from the consequences of your own sin and bad choices?

Reflections, curiosities, frustrations:

Study 16

Strength in the Face of Desolation and Saul's Cowardly Death

Read 1 Samuel 30-31

Observation Questions

1. What happens to David's wives?

2. What is David's conversation with the Lord in chapter 30, verses 7-8?

3. How does David defeat the Amalekites? What is restored to him when he does?

4. How does Saul die? Who else dies with him?

Chapter 30

Verses 1-6. How exhausted must David and his men be at this point? Consider what their emotional lives have been like. For months they have been hiding, running, escaping. Then they fought in endless skirmishes while still never seeing their wives and children, who were hidden in Ziklag. Tension built in the ranks while they prepared to follow David into battle with the Philistines to fight their own countrymen. Just as the controlled rage and frustration of the situation must have been about to boil over, Yahweh delivers them and allows them to head, finally, toward their families. The miles must have seemed long but worthwhile, as they knew they were done; finally a break was coming. But as they start to see the first outlines of the city on the horizon, something doesn't look right. Instead of happy children running to welcome them, only the silent black ashes of their empty homes appear as they approach the town. The wives and children they love have been taken, probably to be sold into slavery. David's men have reached their emotional limit. Disappointment and sadness quickly turn to rage, which finds its way into a growing demand for David's death. It is easy at this point to gloss over the end of verse 6 and the little phrase "but David strengthened himself in the LORD his God." David is tired, too, scared and disappointed. But instead of turning inward and becoming bitter, he reminds himself of what he knows is true. The Lord has delivered him time and time again. David may have also recounted the stories of the last few months, remembered Samuel's words to him so long ago, and even sung familiar words that retaught his soul the truth about God. This is the only way out of despair caused by circumstances, meditation on God's character and past faithfulness.

Verses 7-15. And then, he approaches God in his need. David knows the only one who could possibly deliver him is the one who has done so over and over. He uses the usual means of hearing from God in his day, the ephod—a garment worn by the priests and sometimes by David—and God answers him. Not only does God answer with a definite direction in terms of going after the Amalekites, but he also gives David literal direction. Yahweh brings to David a man who could take him to exactly where his enemies had gone. This is no coincidence; it is more of the answer to the prayers of David.

Verses 16-31. Consider the posture of David versus the posture of the troublemakers in his crew that do not want to share the spoils. David understands that everything they have recovered from the Amalekites is a gift from God. Because of this he is not territorial or greedy but generous, an attitude of grace. The wicked men presume that what they have, they have earned and are operating on a philosophy of works, impressed with their own accomplishments. As Davis writes, "The difference between grace and works is the difference between worship and idolatry" (318). How often do we mimic these men's attitudes? We hold something(s) or someone(s) with an iron fist, determined not to lose what we think we have earned, all the while worshipping those things and becoming bound to them. But what freedom comes when we hold the gifts of God with an open hand, thanking him for what he's given, which we surely didn't deserve?

Chapter 31

Verses 1-7. Here we pick up the narrative of the Philistine battle that was begun in the beginning of chapter 29. It's as if the narrator is glad to take a detour and talk about David for awhile. He returns to the battle of Saul and Israel against the Philistines already in progress. Saul is hit and knows that he is dying, probably from a loss of blood. But his armor bearer refuses to kill him, so Saul falls on his own sword. The first king, once brave and valiant as the leader of Israel's army, is dead. This is a tragic moment, as evidenced by the fleeing of the people who are then replaced in their cities by the Philistines. But not all is lost. Although the king is dead and the children of Israel have been scattered, one thing remains—the word of God. Remember that the Lord had said, through Samuel in chapter 15, verse 28, and chapter 28, verse 19, that Saul and his sons would die together. God always fulfills his word. Kings and kingdoms, armies and leaders fail. Only the word of God never, ever fails.

Verses 8–13. It was common for conquering armies to take their enemy's armor and place it in temples. The placement of the army's weapons into a place of subjection in the temple would have signified the defeat of that army's god as well. In this case, the heads of Saul and also his sons were probably passed around to various towns in Philistia like trophies. Their bodies were probably hung from iron hooks on the wall near the entrance to the city, so everyone could see their failure. What a shameful, disappointing end for the first king of God's people. There is one moment of tenderness when the people of Jabesh-Gilead hear of Saul's defeat. In gratitude and remembrance of Saul's rescue from Nahash, they mourn for him and take down his body. It was not the norm for Israelites to burn bodies (Ellicott, 1 Sam. 31:12), but in this case, burying Saul and his sons may have led to their capture, so they burn them and bury their bones honorably.

Originally, 1 and 2 Samuel were all one book, so if we feel like the story has ended abruptly, we only need to continue reading the next book. At the end of 1 Samuel, the sheep of Israel have been scattered like sheep without a shepherd (Davis, 329). But if we keep reading through the history of Israel, we will see, just as we have seen in Saul and Jonathan and David, more and more glimpses of the true shepherd. There is only one leader, one shepherd whose strength, soundness of mind, and word will never fail.

Reflection Questions

5. David and his soldiers must have felt total devastation when they came home to find their homes destroyed and their children and wives captured, and in their grief they wanted to hurt David. Define the word *devastation*. When you have experienced devastation in your own life? How did you respond?

6. The scripture tells us, "But David strengthened himself in the Lord his God." What do you think this means? How would you explain to someone how to go about doing this?

7. God used a young Egyptian man who was a servant to an Amelekite to give specific, extremely helpful details to David so he could go and find the captured wives and children. This man was sick and had been left behind by his master when David stumbled upon him. What a picture of providence. Define *providence*. Tell a story of providence that you have recently experienced.

8. Although some of his men disagreed with him, David divided the spoils among the soldiers who fought in the battle and those that stayed behind, even making this practice a new statute. Do you think this was a fair thing to do? Why or why not?

9. Finally we have arrived at Saul's death fulfilling what God had promised. Once injured, Israel's first king takes his own life, and the people of Israel scatter. What hope are God's people left with and why?

Reflections, curiosities, frustrations:

Acknowledgments

Hope: I would like to thank my husband, who preaches to me the best sermons when I need them most. For my children, Cana, Thea, and Nias, who bring me joy and show me how much I still need to learn. To my parents, who have always given me the gift of unconditional love. TCU Sisters, you have my heart. Ladies of the morning Bible study at Redeemer Church, we are forever in your debt for your trust in us and all our learning curves. And to our awesome editor, Renae, who sees all the little pieces and us in fullness; you have made all of it better!

Chris: To Michael, who was often woken up from a dead sleep with some deep, theological question or accosted with my interpretation arguments with no warning; you are my favorite. To the Redeemer women, you have loved me so well through this process, and your trust of me with your minds and hearts is priceless. And Renae, your encouragement has been just as helpful as your editing.

Bibliography

Clarke, Adam. *Clarke's Commentary on the Bible*. Nashville: Nelson Reference, 1997.

Davis, Dale Ralph. *1 Samuel: Looking on the Heart*. Fearn, Scotland: Christian Focus Publications, 2000.

Ellicott, Charles J. *A Bible Commentary for English Readers*. Charleston, SC: Nabu Press, 2011.

Ellison, H. L. *Joshua-2 Samuel*. Scripture Union Study Books. Grand Rapids, MI: Eerdmans, 1966.

ESV Study Bible. Wheaton, IL: Crossway, 2008.

Expositor's Bible Commentary, volume 3. Grand Rapids, MI: Zondervan, 1976.

Keil, C. F., and F. Delitzsch. *Commentary on the Old Testament*. Hendrickson Publishers, 1996.

Lloyd-Jones, Sally. *The Jesus Storybook Bible*. Grand Rapids, MI: Zondervan, 2007.

Made in the USA
Lexington, KY
05 September 2017